Contents

KU-850-292

A vision of the future

Television has today become an important part of many people's lives across the world. It is taken for granted that, at the flick of a switch, live pictures can be beamed via satellite from one side of the world to the other in a matter of seconds. Television has become such a powerful and persuasive influence in all our lives that it affects the way we live and, in many ways, how we think. It is a vital source of information, for good but also, some people believe, for bad.

We may take television for granted today, but the path to this amazing piece of equipment was very winding, and littered with the frustrations and shattered dreams of many inventors. The word 'television' comes from the Greek word *tele* (far) and the Latin word *videre* (to see). The idea of sending pictures from one place to another was first seriously thought of in 1878, when the Italian scientist de Paiva presented his ideas of television or 'distant vision'. But it was not until 47 years later that Scottish engineer and inventor John Logie Baird gave the first public demonstration of television before an amazed world.

A photograph of John Logie Baird taken in 1925. This was the year in which he made the first television transmission of the human face.

*This modern, flat **plasma** screen television is one of the latest versions of the invention that John Logie Baird developed early in the 20th century.*

Baird's genius

It was Baird who turned the dream into reality. A number of other people were working on television at the same time as Baird. When he started his work, all the basic tools he needed had already been invented. But it was his genius that enabled him to put all the parts of the jigsaw together and make television work. It is difficult for us today to appreciate the huge impact television has had on all our lives, as a source of information as well as entertainment. Until the appearance of television, people relied upon live shows, cinema and radio as the main sources of entertainment and information. Television brought all this into people's homes.

John Logie Baird's life story is a very moving one. He struggled for most of his life against ill health, poverty and many disappointments to achieve his dream. He started many different ventures and came up with a number of inventions, but it was television that made his name in history. It was his courage and determination against all odds that led him to the breakthrough that would change the world for ever. He achieved fame for his work but no fortune, and was finally cheated by an early death.

Early life

John Logie Baird was born on 13 August 1888, in the town of Helensburgh on the west coast of Scotland. He was the fourth child of a **Presbyterian Church** minister – the Reverend John Baird – and his wife Jessie. There were two older sisters and a brother. Their father was a large, strict man with eccentric habits. The children had a deeply religious upbringing and the family led a quiet and modest life in a large, square, stone house. There was little money to spend on amusements. In those days there was no radio or television and the telephone was still an expensive piece of equipment that only the rich could afford.

A rich imagination

Although there was little in the way of entertainment in the family home, young John had a rich and vivid imagination. The older he became, the more his imagination and inventiveness grew with him. At the age of 2, he developed a near-fatal illness. This was the first of many illnesses that were to plague him throughout his life, upsetting many of his plans and opportunities.

A view of the River Clyde and the town of Helensburgh in Scotland near the end of the 19th century. John Logie Baird lived here until the age of 21.

John Logie Baird's parents, the Reverend John Baird (left) and his wife Jessie. (The identity of the person in the middle is unknown.) They provided their children with a strict but happy upbringing.

JESSIE BAIRD

John Logie Baird's mother was born Jessie Morrison Inglis and came from a prosperous Glasgow shipbuilding family. She was in her early twenties when she met her future husband. Once they were married, she took her duties as a Church minister's wife very seriously. Baird wrote many years later: 'Of my mother I find it difficult to write. She was the one experience I had of unselfish devotion. Her whole life was taken up in looking after others …'

John's first school, Ardenlee, was run by a strict headmaster, Mr Porteous. Mr Porteous kept control of the classroom with his cane which, Baird was to write later, he used 'vigorously and indiscriminately'. John, however, was placed in another class. Here he was able to enjoy his lessons and quickly learned to read and write. Despite his poor health, he was an energetic boy and was popular with his classmates.

Mr Porteous soon went bankrupt and John was sent to another school, run by the fearsome Miss Johnson. She was even more strict than Mr Porteous, and Baird was later to describe his time at her school as 'the most miserable time. I was terrorized and the years spent at that school are among the most unhappy of my life.'

Growing interests

The **Industrial Revolution** was at its height in Europe when John was growing up. It was a time of great industrial production, when inventions such as the telephone were changing the world. The British author H.G. Wells inspired the young John with his visions of the future.

New experiments

Outside school, John's imagination helped him develop his scientific interests. His first great interest was in telephones, which had been invented by fellow Scot Alexander Graham Bell twelve years before John's birth, in 1876. John set up his own personal **telephone exchange** in his bedroom at home and connected wires to the houses of four of his friends. When the National Telephone Company found out about this, they quickly put an end to it!

Another early enthusiasm of John's was for electrical engineering. He soon wired up the family home for electric light, with a home-made generator in a building next door. A small water wheel under the kitchen sink powered a set of batteries.

Although John had poor health as a boy, and strict teachers made him miserable during his school days, he was a quick learner and enjoyed reading.

The famous author H.G. Wells, whose books inspired Baird as a boy.

H.G. WELLS

The writings of Herbert George Wells (1866–1946) had a great influence on Baird when he was at school. Wells was one of the most important popular authors since Charles Dickens. He made his name in the 1890s with novels about the possibilities of scientific discovery, such as *The Time Machine* (1895) and *The War of the Worlds* (1898). These were the books that made such an impression on Baird. The two met by chance when they were both sailing to New York in 1931. But Baird was very disappointed by his hero and described their meeting as 'a great anti-climax'.

Cold showers

In 1898, when John was 10 years old, he was sent to a new and bigger school called the Larchfield Academy. Here, Latin and Greek were considered much more important than science and mathematics. Sport was also very important, and after every game the boys had to take a cold shower. In the 1930s Baird said in a newspaper interview: 'I believe that most of the ill health which has interrupted my work has been caused by too much cold water in my school days. The shower baths helped undermine my already delicate constitution.'

During his time at Larchfield, John became very interested in photography. He saved hard to buy his first camera and was soon elected president of the school Photographic Society. To his great disappointment, the society was eventually closed down.

A move to college

It was now clear that John's real interests lay in scientific experiment. He began to do some research that he would later use in his television work.

Clear ideas

Baird tried to keep up with the latest inventions and discoveries, such as that made in 1873 by the British scientist Joseph May of the light-sensitive properties of an **element** called selenium. Baird made many experiments using selenium: 'I did learn one thing, which was that the current from a selenium cell was infinitesimally small. Before anything could be done, some means of amplifying this must be found. I made all sorts of attempts at amplifiers but could get nothing sufficiently sensitive.' This problem would eventually be solved when John Fleming and later Lee de Forest invented their **amplifying valves**.

With his scientific interests and abilities now firmly established, Baird left Larchfield at the age of 18 in 1906, and went on to the Royal Technical College in Glasgow. Britain had led the world in the **Industrial Revolution** throughout the 19th century, and Glasgow was one of the most important centres of its development.

Baird (on the left) with one of his cousins in 1906. They are riding a type of motorbike nicknamed by the local people 'the Baird Reaper and Binder'.

Baird began a course in electrical engineering and soon settled into his studies at the college. He enjoyed the work and did well, but his constant bouts of ill health meant that he took eight years instead of three to gain his **diploma** in electrical engineering.

In 1909, at the age of 21, as part of his course Baird started working as an **apprentice** in local engineering companies. He lived in Glasgow, returning home at weekends. The poor working conditions he experienced turned him into a life-long **socialist** and increased his steely determination to succeed. He wrote later: 'The years of romance and youth were lost in sordid and mean lodgings, in soul destroying surroundings, under grey skies … What a wave of resentment and anger comes over me, even now, when I think of the awful conditions of work in those Glasgow factories – the sodden gloom, the bitter, bleak, cold rain, the slave-driven workers cooped in a vile atmosphere with the incessant roar and clatter of machinery from six in the morning to six at night …'

The Royal Technical College in Glasgow, which Baird attended from 1906 to 1914.

In a cousin's words:

'His head appeared always in the clouds. When his name was mentioned, relatives would smile and shrug, saying, "puir Johnnie, puir Johnnie." However, we had to admit that he had the last laugh. He knew what he wanted and he achieved it.'

Early career

In 1914, at the age of 25, Baird finally received his **Associateship** and **Diploma** in Electrical Engineering. He now had the chance to enrol on a six-month course to study for a Bachelor of Science degree at the University of Glasgow.

Out in the world

Baird's brief spell at university was one of the happiest times of his life. He wrote: 'I had the sense not to endeavour to cram and did the absolute minimum of work, while heartily enjoying the society of my fellow students. We had innumerable outings in the happy atmosphere that can only be found among students.'

However, Baird started at university just before the First World War erupted in August 1914. In March 1915 he left university without taking his final examinations. Like most young men of the time, he volunteered for military service. But he was turned down because of his poor health: 'The medical examiner … examined my skinny form with sad and disapproving eyes, tapping my scanty chest and placed his ear to listen to my wheezy breathing.'

Baird at the Rutherglen (Glasgow) station of the Clyde Valley Power Company in 1915. His health was badly affected while he was working there.

After several months of seeking work, Baird was eventually accepted as an assistant mains electrical engineer with the Clyde Valley Electrical Power Company. Once again, he found himself working in cold, gloomy conditions.

Success with socks

In his spare time, Baird started a number of small business ventures. One that was reasonably successful was the Baird Undersock business. He devised a way of treating the underside of socks with a substance called borax to keep feet warm and dry. He was a 'one-man business'. He treated the socks at night and then sold them to shops the following day.

In 1919 Baird resigned from his job. He was now 30 years old and the sock business was doing so well that he was making £200 a week – an enormous sum for those days. But his old enemy, poor health, was lurking round the corner. Another bad cold kept him in bed for weeks and he eventually had to close down his sock business.

> **In Baird's words:**
>
> *'Sordid, miserable work, punctuated by repeated colds and influenza. I wanted more money. I got 30 shillings a week and I was unable to get a better job because I was always ill. Finally I decided it was hopeless and I had better try and start some business which was less strenuous and in which I would be my own master.'*
>
> (From Baird's autobiographical notes, *Sermons, Soap and Television*)

Baird employed a team of women to carry around boards which advertised his undersock business.

Determined to win

With every plan he made, Baird seemed to be thwarted by his health. When his sock business failed, he decided to leave the cold, damp climate of the British Isles. He sold the remains of the business for £1600 and set sail for Trinidad in the West Indies in the winter of 1919. Baird had plans to set up a new business importing goods from Europe.

Shattered dreams

'I was going to live in the land of the humming bird, to spend my days and nights free from all cares and in equatorial paradise,' wrote Baird. But this vision of paradise quickly turned into a nightmare. Port of Spain, the capital of Trinidad, was full of businesses similar to Baird's and he found it impossible to sell any of his goods. A few weeks after his arrival, he fell seriously ill with **malaria**. He was making no money and the profit he had made from his sock business was quickly disappearing.

Lying in bed with fever, Baird realized he had to make some money, and fast. As both fruit and sugar grew in Trinidad, he came up with the idea of starting a jam factory. As soon as he was well enough to work again, he set up his jam-making business in the Santa Cruz Valley. He hired an assistant and together they started making jam in enormous copper pots. But immediately, their small jam factory was invaded by thousands of insects attracted by the sweet smell. After struggling on for nearly a year, Baird was finally forced to close the factory down when he fell ill with another bout of malaria.

Baird's jam factory in Trinidad.

Breakdown

In September 1920 Baird sold the jam business and returned to Britain. He moved to London and set up yet another business, this time selling soap. He was just beginning to make a profit from this when he had a complete mental and

The town of Hastings on the south coast of England. Baird moved here in 1922 to improve his health. It remained his home for two years and he did some of his most important work here.

physical breakdown. His doctor advised him to leave the business world altogether and move as far south in England as possible.

So it was, in late 1922, that Baird moved to the seaside town of Hastings on the south coast of England. He was now 34 years old and utterly exhausted. He had no job prospects and little money. The future looked bleak, but Baird was about to enter one of the most remarkable and creative periods of his life.

15

Inventions before Baird

Although Baird had long been involved in many varied business ventures, he had always managed to keep up an interest in the transmission of pictures. Soon after his arrival in Hastings, he returned to the ideas and experiments that he had started in Scotland. Scientists had already made a number of inventions and discoveries that laid the foundations for Baird's work on television.

Radio waves

Unlike the telephone or telegraph, radio and television do not need wires to transmit signals. During the 19th century, scientists began thinking that magnetic and electrical effects were transmitted in waves, like light. In 1885 the German scientist Heinrich Hertz (1857–94) proved this was the case. He showed that **electromagnetic waves** emitted by an electric spark on one side of his laboratory could be picked up by a wire on the other side. This proved the existence of a type of waves later called **radio waves**.

Guglielmo Marconi with his wireless telegraph. Marconi's success in sending radio signals across the Atlantic at the beginning of the century would be an inspiration to Baird.

Sending messages over the air

In 1894 the Italian scientist Guglielmo Marconi (1874–1937) carried out further experiments, with similar equipment to Hertz's. He pressed a button that was 9 metres away from a bell but not connected to it by wire, and made the bell ring. After improving his equipment, Marconi was able to send a message in **Morse code** from England to a radio receiver 50 kilometres (31 miles) away in France. In 1901 he sent out the first radio signals across the Atlantic Ocean, from England to Canada. Five years later, a Canadian scientist, Reginald Fessenden, made the first radio transmission of the human voice.

Spinning discs

In 1884 the German engineer Paul Nipkow (1860–1940) designed a disc with a spiral pattern of holes cut into it. When one of these discs, known as **Nipkow discs**, was rotated quickly in front of an object, light from the object passed through the holes. These flashes of light were sent through another Nipkow disc, which reproduced them on a screen as an exact image of the original object. This was an important step in the development of the television.

Without the invention of two kinds of **amplifying valves**, radio and television would not have been possible. In 1904 the British engineer John Fleming (1849–1945) invented the **diode valve**. This allowed the transmission of electrical signals over long distances. Two years later, in 1906, an American, Lee de Forest (1873–1961), invented the triode valve. This was used to amplify electrical signals so that they could be transmitted over even greater distances.

Diagram illustrating the principle of the Nipkow disc.

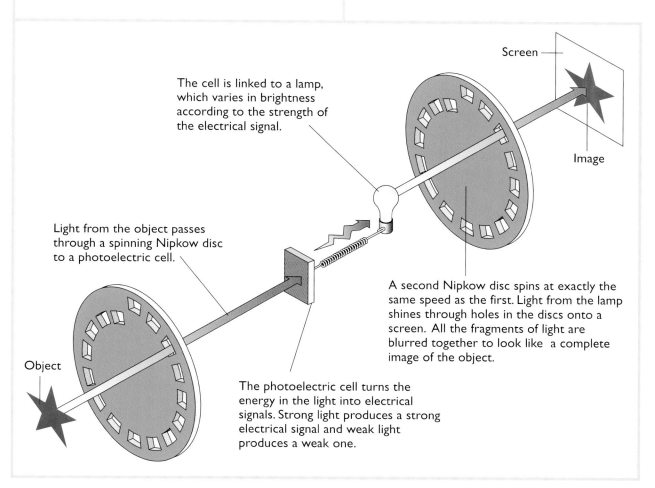

Screen

The cell is linked to a lamp, which varies in brightness according to the strength of the electrical signal.

Image

Light from the object passes through a spinning Nipkow disc to a photoelectric cell.

A second Nipkow disc spins at exactly the same speed as the first. Light from the lamp shines through holes in the discs onto a screen. All the fragments of light are blurred together to look like a complete image of the object.

Object

The photoelectric cell turns the energy in the light into electrical signals. Strong light produces a strong electrical signal and weak light produces a weak one.

An important breakthrough

When Baird arrived in Hastings in 1922, he went for long, bracing walks along the coast and slowly recovered his health. His thoughts turned more and more to television. A number of new inventions, such as **amplifying valves**, made the possibility more real.

Old interests return

At this time, Baird was sharing rooms at 21 Linton Crescent, Hastings, with his childhood friend Guy Robertson. As he began his new experiments on television, so the rooms began to fill up with electrical equipment, until Baird decided he needed more space. For five shillings (twenty-five pence) a week he rented a small attic room above a flower shop in Queen's Avenue. This became his laboratory and, by late 1923, he had built his first crude television **transmitter**. Robertson helped him put together this strange-looking machine. There was no spare money, so they used various bits and pieces, such as a tea chest, discs made from an old hat box, and a knitting needle. The base was made from an old coffin lid!

The cinema owner and businessman William Day, who became Baird's first financial backer.

Charles Francis Jenkins, who worked on the development of the television at about the same time as Baird, although the two did not know of each other's work.

At last the machine was ready for testing. Some of Baird's other helpers – known as 'Baird's Boys' – were present when the machine was switched on. One, Victor Mills, placed his hand in front of the rotating disc and a small, flickering image of his hand was projected on to a screen. Everyone in the room was amazed. After all the chaos of the preceding months, Baird had shown with this strange machine that television really could work.

However, Baird knew that he had to achieve a much clearer image. In order to do this he would need better equipment, which would cost money. Eventually, he received some money from his family, and also £200 from a Hastings cinema owner, William Day, who became his first backer.

CHARLES JENKINS

Some months before the events in Hastings, an American called Charles Francis Jenkins (1867–1934) had been experimenting along the same lines as Baird. Jenkins, however, did not achieve any results until many months after Baird's success. Although some historians cannot now agree on who was first, it is certain that neither inventor knew of the other's work at the time. Jenkins was a physicist and inventor born near Dayton in Ohio, USA. In 1894 he suggested the possibility of transmitting pictures electrically over a distance. During the 1920s he gave many demonstrations of **mechanical television**, using both **Nipkow discs** and a system of his own based on rotating glass discs.

Return to London

Baird photographed in 1924 sitting behind his transmitting equipment which uses a large **Nipkow disc**.

A report in the *Hastings and St Leonard's Observer*, 26 July 1924, stated: 'Mr J. L. Baird, who claims to be the inventor of television (seeing by wireless) met with an accident whilst carrying out experiments in his workshop in Queen's Avenue on Thursday. A loud explosion was heard and Mr Baird was found lying helpless on the floor ... Mr Baird's hands were badly burned and he was much shaken. The apparatus was damaged.'

Baird's landlord was furious. He gave Baird an ultimatum – either stop the experiments, or leave his rooms. Baird had no intention of stopping, so he packed his bags and went.

A new chapter

When Baird had left London for Hastings two years earlier, he had been a very sick man with no idea of what the future might hold. Now, he was much more certain of where he was going and knew that he should return to London. He rented two attic rooms at 22 Frith Street in Soho for his laboratory, and found lodgings in Ealing, West London.

Baird worked extremely hard over the next two years on improving his **transmitter**. He was very short of money, and he wrote later that these months were some of his most difficult of his life.

Baird needed more publicity and money to take his work further. He had shown that television had a future, but he found it extremely difficult to get people to invest their money in it. Eventually, Mr Gordon Selfridge, the owner of the famous London department store, offered Baird £20 a week for three weeks to demonstrate his television equipment in Selfridge's.

A television picture is made up of hundreds of lines. A tiny spot of light flashes along each line at 52 millionths of a second per line. This is too fast for the human eye to notice, so that the lines merge together to make up a complete picture on the screen. The more lines there are, the clearer the picture. Early pictures were made up of 30 lines, while pictures today consist of 625 lines.

This offer came at just the right time for Baird, but his equipment often let him down. People now began to doubt his ability to improve the transmitter. Even William Day, his first backer, stopped giving him money. Baird was working longer and longer hours, sometimes through the night. He could hardly afford to feed himself, let alone buy new equipment. As a result, his health suffered once again and he was on the point of giving up altogether.

Selfridge's, the department store in London where Baird gave public demonstrations of his television equipment. This generated interest in his work.

A public demonstration

Depressed and unable to see a way out of his situation, Baird appealed to his family for help. His mother's family bought £500-worth of shares in his business. At last Baird could buy the equipment he desperately needed to build a new, more light-sensitive **transmitter**.

Success at last!

On 2 October 1925, Baird tried out his new television equipment. He placed a ventriloquist's dummy, nicknamed Bill, in front of the transmitting disc. To his relief and delight, a clear black-and-white picture of Bill's face appeared on a screen in the room next door. This was the result he had been working so hard to achieve. In a burst of excitement, he rushed out of his rooms to the offices below and dragged a startled office boy called William Taynton upstairs. He pushed the boy into a chair in front of the television camera and then ran next door to look at the receiver screen. There was the face of William Taynton, the first person ever to appear on television!

Baird knew that having got this far, he had to move quickly as there were rivals closing in on his tail, especially in America. On 27 January 1926, Baird gave a demonstration in his Soho laboratory to 40 members of the **Royal Institution**. They all crowded into the tiny rooms and were spellbound as the images flickered across the screen.

Baird's first successful transmitting equipment. The head of Bill the ventriloquist's dummy can be seen on the left.

News of Baird's success spread all round the country and beyond. However, Baird still had much more work to do to improve the picture's **definition** and increase the distance over which it could be transmitted. He became alarmed when a team of Americans announced that they planned to transmit pictures by telephone line from New York to Washington, a distance of more than 322 kilometres (200 miles).

With the help of his new business manager, Oliver Hutchinson, Baird moved into more spacious rooms near Leicester Square. He also hired a technical assistant. He applied to the Post Office and, in early 1927, was granted the first-ever television transmitting licence, number 2 TV.

CAPTAIN HUTCHINSON

Oliver Hutchinson had originally been a rival of Baird's in the soap business. In 1926, by chance the paths of the two men crossed again and Hutchinson agreed to take over the business side of Baird's work. Hutchinson was a very cautious man. However, he was successful in raising extra money for the company, which enabled Baird to carry on with his experiments.

A new era

The Baird Television Company was formed in April 1927. The next day the morning's newspapers carried the headlines that the American Telegraph and Telephone Company had given a demonstration in New York called 'Television at Last'. The competition was rapidly catching up with Baird. He now had to work even faster than before if he wanted to stay ahead. His American rivals had the backing of rich and powerful companies, whereas he was practically working on his own.

Keeping ahead

The race was now really on and Baird concentrated on the performance of his television system. Following the American success in sending pictures by wire from New York to Washington in April 1927, Baird was determined to top them. 'If distance makes headlines, I can do better,' he said. In May 1927 he transmitted a picture from London to Glasgow, a distance of 705 kilometres (438 miles).

Baird standing beside a device called an infra-red Noctovisor.

Seeing in the dark

At this time, Baird was also developing a system in which he used infra-red light instead of his former dazzling blaze of electric light. This system, which he called 'Noctovision', was so effective that it was even able to 'see' in the dark and through fog. Baird also started working on colour television at this time.

That same year, the Television Society was founded and Baird's work was being taken much more seriously. His name was also becoming widely known to the public. But strains were appearing in his working relationship with Hutchinson, as Baird found him too cautious. Baird was introduced to a financial journalist called Sidney Mosely, who was much more aware than Hutchinson of the power of publicity. He soon replaced Hutchinson as Baird's business manager. He was very successful in using his writing skills to produce regular publicity reports on Baird's successes.

THE BBC

Despite Baird's success in 1927, he still had to convince important organizations of the uses of television if he wanted to make further progress. The most important of these organizations was the British Broadcasting Corporation (BBC), which held a **monopoly** on broadcasting transmissions. The BBC was founded in 1922 and, under its Director-General Sir John Reith, had very high standards of quality in radio transmissions. It considered Baird's television pictures not good enough for regular transmissions. Baird's business manager Sidney Mosely tried to persuade the BBC to **broadcast** Baird's television system. He even wrote to newspapers and members of parliament to try and win their backing. But it was to be some time yet before the BBC finally agreed.

The BBC headquarters at Broadcasting House in London. Baird always had a very uneasy working relationship with the BBC.

25

New ideas

During 1928 Baird was working on a number of new and exciting projects. At the end of the previous year, the Baird Television Company had moved to larger premises in Long Acre, Covent Garden, where Baird could carry out his experiments in greater comfort.

More successes

On 9 February 1928, Baird achieved another great success. A few months before, he had sent his assistant Ben Clapp to America. Baird had always wanted to be the first person to send television pictures from England to North America. He would be following in the footsteps of his hero, Guglielmo Marconi, who, in 1901, had sent the first radio

Baird (on the left) and his first business manager, Oliver Hutchinson, fixing a television aerial on the roof of their offices in Long Acre, London.

signals across the Atlantic. Baird set up his television **transmitter** '2 TV'. He sent image signals of Bill the ventriloquist's dummy by telephone line to a receiving station in Coulsdon, Surrey. From there the signals were sent 4828 kilometres (3000 miles) across the Atlantic to Hartsdale, near New York. Here they were received by Ben Clapp, who managed to tune the doll's features clearly on the receiver. The television screen went blank for a while, but was then filled with the head of Baird himself who was televised for about half an hour.

This was the first time that a picture had been transmitted so far. American viewers were amazed by what they saw, and Baird's name became famous throughout North America.

As these successes were taking place, Baird continued with his other work. This included the development of a camera that could be used in ordinary daylight, and a successful demonstration of colour television. In this, he showed a bowl of brightly coloured flowers and a white basket containing red strawberries. Another amazing achievement was 'Phonovision', in which sound and pictures were recorded on a disc.

In the words of two American newspapers:

'Baird was the first to achieve television at all, over any distance. Now he must be credited with having been the first to disembody the human form optically and electrically, flash it ... across the ocean and then reassemble it for American eyes. His success deserves to rank with Marconi's sending of the letter "S" across the Atlantic ...'

(The New York Times, the morning after Baird's demonstration in 1928)

'It is said that probably one thousand engineers and laboratory men were involved in the American test between Washington and New York ... only a dozen worked with Baird!'

(The New York Herald Tribune)

A 'disc model' television, developed by Baird in the 1930s.

Forging ahead

Baird had succeeded in sorting out the early basic problems in television. He had added to this success with his other experiments in colour television and recording pictures. But he still had a struggle on his hands. In order to make television successful, he had to win the support of the broadcasters, and that meant the BBC.

Another challenge

In 1928 Baird built a television receiving set and demonstrated it at the National Radio Exhibition in London. It had a small glass screen and was contained in a large wooden cabinet. Although it worked well, it was large and bulky. One visitor to the exhibition, Percy Packman, was an engineer at the Plessey electrical company. He offered to make improvements to Baird's set. Baird was very pleased with the result, which was neater and lighter, and the Plessey Company was given the contract to build the world's first mass-produced television sets. One thousand of these, known as 'televisors', were built between 1929 and 1931.

The National Radio Exhibition of 1928, where Baird showed the prototype for his factory-made television set, called the 'televisor'.

A Baird 'televisor', the first mass-produced television set.

Everything seemed to be going well for Baird and his television. But he now realized that he had to prove its success in public. To do this he had to work with the BBC. Engineers at the BBC were still not very impressed by the quality of Baird's pictures. Sidney Mosely contacted everyone he could to try and bring the BBC round. But relations between Baird and the BBC were strained. The situation was not helped by the fact that he also did not get on with the Director-General, Sir John Reith.

Eventually, the **Postmaster General**, Sir William Mitchell-Thompson, was given a demonstration of Baird's television. He was so impressed that he suggested to the BBC that it should begin regular television **broadcasts**. But still the BBC refused. However, at last the BBC agreed to try out the system and, on 30 September 1929, the first television broadcast went out from Baird's studio in Covent Garden. This was done for a short period each day. Sometimes the pictures were good, sometimes not so good.

JOHN REITH

John Reith (1889–1971) was the first Director-General of the BBC, from 1927 until 1938. He was a tall, powerful man with a very strong personality and he insisted on very high standards. He had been a fellow student of Baird's at the Royal Technical College in Glasgow, where he trained as a civil engineer. The two had not liked each other even then. Reith later became a government minister and was made Lord Reith in 1940.

Rival systems

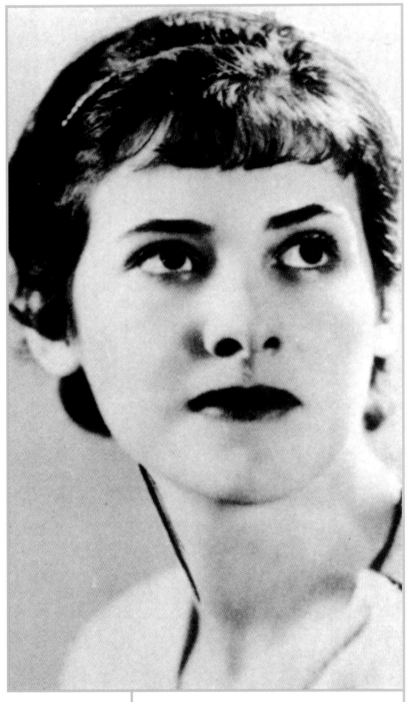

The South African concert pianist Margaret Albu. This photograph was taken at the time of her marriage to Baird in 1931.

In September 1931 Baird and Mosely set sail on the liner *Aquitania* from Southampton to New York. The Baird Television Company was going bankrupt as the backers were seeing no return on their investments and were unwilling to invest yet more money.

Baird had always received enthusiastic press coverage in the USA. Mosely now believed that the North American continent, with its thousands of potential television viewers, offered the best chance of saving the company's fortunes.

All change

Baird arrived in New York to a tremendous welcome. However, despite a lot of valuable publicity from the newspapers, the trip was not a success. The Radio Corporation of America (RCA) appealed against a decision to allow Baird to televise in the USA. After three months, Baird returned to England empty-handed.

Margaret Albu

Another important event during his American trip was Baird's marriage in New York to a concert pianist called Margaret Cecilia Albu, on 13 November 1931. Margaret Albu was born in 1907 in Johannesburg, South Africa, the daughter of a South African businessman and an English mother. She became an accomplished pianist and in 1925 was sent to London to complete her music studies. She met Baird there in 1930. He was 43, nineteen years older than her, but they were to have a happy marriage, Margaret supporting her husband through all his difficulties and disappointments. Their first child, Diana, was born in September 1932.

At this time, events in the world of television were changing fast. **Electronic television** was catching up and now posed a much greater threat to Baird's mechanical system than anything before.

Baird holding a large cathode ray tube from a television set. This formed the basis of the electronic television system which replaced Baird's mechanical system.

ELECTRONIC TELEVISION

In 1908, the Scottish electrical engineer Campbell Swinton published his ideas on using electrons to make television work. Some of the equipment, such as **cathode ray tubes**, had already been invented, but Swinton could not see how his theories could be put to practical use.

In 1907 a Russian scientist called Boris Rosing demonstrated a simple television system using a mechanical camera and a cathode ray receiver. But this device could only show basic black-and-white outlines with no light or shade. One of Rosing's students was Vladimir Zworykin, who emigrated to the USA in 1917. He invented a device called an **iconoscope** in 1923, which solved Swinton's problem of the electronic camera. It was an electronic device with a lens that focused an image onto a screen inside a glass tube.

Catching up

The same year as Baird's trip to the USA, 1931, two of Britain's leading record companies merged to form Electric and Musical Industries (EMI). Immediately, the new company decided to concentrate on television research. In 1932 it was granted a **patent** on an electronic camera tube called the 'Emitron', based on the Russian scientist Vladimir Zworykin's **iconoscope**. Shortly afterwards, the EMI engineers joined forces with those in another electrical company, Marconi. These were now the forces ranged against Baird's **mechanical television** system.

The television camera with the Emitron camera tube (right), which was patented by EMI in 1932.

A battle for supremacy

For the moment, Baird was still ahead in the race. The BBC was at last becoming more interested in the possibilities of a nation-wide television service. There was still much more work to be done, but the BBC could see where things were heading and it did not want to be left behind. On 22 August 1932, the first official BBC **broadcast** in Britain took place.

The mirror-drum

In 1931 Baird had designed a new television camera to improve the picture quality. He replaced the spinning **Nipkow discs** with a mirror-drum. A rotating drum was fitted with a series of mirrors, one for each line, and each one tilted at a slight angle to the next. As a beam of light was shone into the camera, it hit the first mirror and was reflected down the picture. The second mirror, slightly tilted away from the first, made the reflected light sweep down the picture slightly to the left of the first one. Each mirror traced out a line until the complete set had covered the entire picture area.

Diagram of a mirror-drum. After Baird invented this in 1931, television pictures became clearer.

The EMI system

All this time, however, the rival electronic system was catching up. In 1934 EMI unveiled its new, all-electronic system, which was a direct challenge to Baird's system. The more lines that divided up the picture, the clearer the result. Baird's pictures had gone from 30 lines per picture to 240, with the use of a mirror-drum. EMI's pictures had 405 lines.

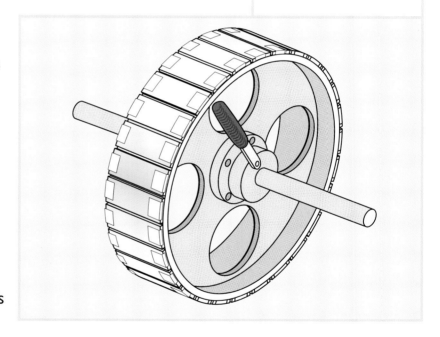

Public interest in television was growing and the number of television sets in use was increasing every month. Eventually, the gap was closed between mechanical and **electronic television**. The time had come for the government to decide which of the two systems should be used for the national television service. In 1934 a **Royal Commission** was set up under the chairmanship of Lord Selsdon (formerly the **Postmaster General**, Sir William Mitchell-Thompson) to look at the future of television broadcasting in Britain.

Decisions

Baird with his 240-line television set on the day the Alexandra Palace trials were announced in 1935.

In April 1935 the Selsdon Commission finally published its report. The result was a bit of an anti-climax. It recommended that there should be a public television service run by the BBC. It suggested that the television service should operate over a trial period, alternating between the Baird system one week and the Marconi-EMI system the next. Once the trial period was complete, only then would enough be known to decide between the two. Television sets were adapted so that they could switch from one to the other. Another important event of 1935 was the birth of John and Margaret's second child, Malcolm, in July.

The final battle

Immediately, the BBC started building a new television centre at Alexandra Palace in north London. Two studios had to be built, one for each system. All the necessary equipment was brought in, dressing rooms prepared for the artists and scenery built. Everything had to be planned and prepared for the world's first **high-definition** television station.

Large-screen TV

As all this work was being done, Baird continued with his own experimental work on colour television and large-screen presentations. On 28 July 1930 he had demonstrated a large-screen picture in the Coliseum Theatre, in London. In August 1936, the Olympic Games were held in Berlin in Germany and were **broadcast** by the German Post Office, using mirror-drum cameras similar to Baird's.

Disaster

Finally, at 3pm on 2 November 1936, the new BBC television service was officially opened at Alexandra Palace. For Baird this was the culmination of all his dreams. But towards the end of the year, the bad luck that had dogged him throughout his life struck once again. On 30 November, just a few weeks after the triumphant opening ceremony, a disastrous fire broke out at Crystal Palace, where Baird had his laboratory, and the huge building was burned to the ground. The laboratory and everything in it were completely destroyed.

With all his equipment and research papers gone, Baird found it practically impossible to maintain a good service from Alexandra Palace. Another problem was that his huge, bulky cameras could not be wheeled around the studios like the lighter Marconi-EMI cameras. In February 1937 the BBC announced that it had decided to use the Marconi-EMI electronic system for all future broadcasts and Baird's mechanical system would be shut down completely. Ruin seemed to be staring Baird in the face.

Alexandra Palace in north London. Located high up on a hill, in 1936 this became the first high-definition television station.

Picking himself up again

Baird was devastated by the BBC's decision to choose the **electronic television** system. But he was not going to let this latest set-back beat him. It was not long before he was back on his feet again, brimming with ideas and plans.

New plans

Baird now decided that his future lay with large-screen television in cinemas and theatres. He already had large-screen television installed in the Dominion Theatre in London. However, he was unable to persuade the cinema owners to take part. So, Baird had to think again. In order to make money, his new company started building television sets designed to receive the Marconi-EMI system. This must have been humiliating for him, but he was a realist, and this side of his business did very well. He was soon employing 500 people to build the sets. By 1939 there were television sets in 20,000 homes in Britain.

A broadcasting session taking place in the Marconi-EMI studio at Alexandra Palace in August 1936.

With the success of his company, Baird now had the time and money to return to some of his earlier projects, especially three-dimensional television and colour television. But he failed to notice that Europe was slipping towards another war.

Baird in the garage of his house in Sydenham. He is sitting in front of the first three-dimensional colour television set.

When the Second World War broke out in September 1939, all television **broadcasting** was immediately shut down. It was considered to be a danger to national security – television signals could be easily picked up by enemy bombers. When the television service shut down, Baird's television factory also had to close.

Another difficult chapter now began in Baird's life. Because of the enemy bombing of London, many women and children were being **evacuated** from the city. John's wife, Margaret, and their two young children were among them. Baird stayed on in the family home in Sydenham, South London. His money was running out and he suffered from his usual bouts of poor health. When his house was hit by a bomb, he moved into a succession of cheap hotels.

Colour and Super TV

Despite everything, this was one of Baird's most productive periods. In the winter of 1940 he took out a patent for his design for a two-colour camera he called a 'Telechrome'. Later, he designed a 600-line colour television and a 'Super TV' set with a screen 0.9 metre wide. Baird was now producing the clearest television pictures he had ever achieved, but he would have to wait until the end of the war before he could show them to the world.

The final disappointment

John Logie Baird in 1941. In spite of constant poor health, poverty, and having his house bombed during the war, Baird was going through a very productive period.

In May 1945 the Second World War in Europe at last came to an end. The news Baird had been longing to hear eventually came through – the BBC was going to start **broadcasting** its television service again from June 1946.

Shaping the future

The British government had invited Baird to join a committee set up in 1944, to give advice on the form the national television service should take after the war. He recommended that the 405-line system that had been in use just before the war should be continued until a new one could take over. He also suggested that the new service should aim to achieve a 1000-line **definition** system, in 3-D and in colour.

As Baird was the only person at this time who was able to demonstrate all these features, it looked as though he would be playing a vital part in post-war television. It seemed that at long last his time had come. He had by now run through all his savings and, as so often in the past, he was very poor. He believed that his Super TV system would be the answer and bring him some of the fortune that had so far eluded him.

Full of excitement and optimism for the future, Baird worked on the finishing touches to his Super TV set. He planned to give a demonstration of the system with coverage of the great victory parade through the streets of London in June 1946. The new system would give pictures of a clarity no one had seen before.

The end of the struggle

All was set, but fate now dealt its cruellest blow of all. On the very day that Baird was to give his demonstration, he was struck down by another illness. His assistants had to go ahead with the demonstration without him. This time it was something much more serious than his usual attacks of influenza – **pneumonia**. Just one week after the successful demonstration of his Super TV, and on the brink of possibly his greatest success of all, on 14 June 1946, John Logie Baird died. He was 58 years old. His widow, Margaret, who had supported him through so many of his ups and downs, took his body back to his birthplace of Helensburgh in Scotland and there he was buried in a small graveyard. She then returned to South Africa where she became a university lecturer in music.

The victory parade held in London in 1946 to celebrate the end of the Second World War. Baird planned to televise the parade but fell ill.

Baird's legacy

A family enjoying an early television set. At first, there were only a few thousand sets – now millions of people all over the world own them.

Ill health had once again cheated Baird of the success he deserved. Margaret was left just £7370 at his death. She claimed that her husband had made more money from his invention of feet-warming socks than he ever did from television. When he died, Baird was leading the world in colour television, but his electronic colour television system was never marketed. His story is one of incredible misfortune that was faced with great courage and determination. Whenever he was knocked down, he bounced back up again.

It is not strictly true to say that Baird invented television, as a number of other people were also working on it at the time. Baird's television system was also not the one that was finally chosen. But it was Baird who led the way in television, and Baird who had the courage, imagination and determination to bring about its success. He created the spark and had the vision to predict the huge impact that television would have on the world.

Baird himself would probably have been surprised, however, at just how great an impact television really has had on our lives. As a means of communication, its influence has been as great as that of the invention of the printing press in the 15th century. When television first appeared, it seemed incredible that pictures and sound could be sent through the air. Information of every kind is now available to anyone who has access to television.

Television has been a force for good and, some people believe, for evil. People's reputations have been made or destroyed by television. According to your point of view, people are now better informed than they ever have been, or their heads are full of the rubbish that is shown on television. There are many arguments both for and against television, but one thing is clear – its impact has been enormous and it now dominates our lives.

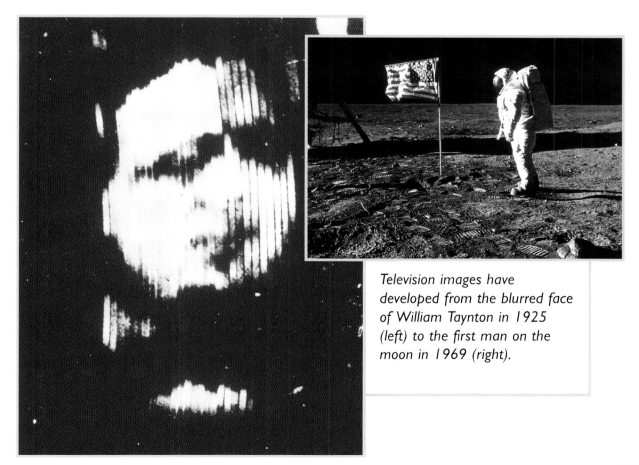

Television images have developed from the blurred face of William Taynton in 1925 (left) to the first man on the moon in 1969 (right).

A television revolution

Security monitor screens.

The television system that is used today is still based upon the electronic system chosen by the BBC in 1937. From the 1950s there was a revolution in television viewing which meant there were sets in millions of homes across the world, with hundreds of companies **broadcasting** to them.

Great advances in technology, especially the invention of the **micro-processor** in 1969, have brought about another revolution in television in recent years. Most television sets today are operated by remote control. Sophisticated but cheap and easy-to-use technology, such as videos and computer games, is now found in many homes. Many stations broadcast screens of text and picture information called *teletext*, and viewers can now shop or choose holidays from the television. We are about to enter an all-digital future, in which **digital televisions** will produce crystal-clear pictures.

A modern digital television set. Slim screens are now replacing the large, bulky sets.

As well as providing entertainment, television technology has many other uses. A thin tube of optical fibres called an *endoscope* allows surgeons to see inside a patient. It carries back an image to a television screen. Television cameras film operations in hospitals, so that medical students can learn by watching them on a television set in another room or building.

ONGOING IMPACT) **Future television**

Hang-on-the-wall televisions appeared in the late 1990s. These have thin, flat **plasma** screens that will gradually replace the bulkier vacuum-tube screens that have been used for more than 60 years. Floor-to-ceiling video screens may be a feature in the homes of the future. By 1998 some computers were able to receive television signals. This marked the beginning of the combination of computers and television. The 'telecomputer' is now a part of many homes, with television, radio and an Internet service all combined in a single unit.

Closed-circuit television (CCTV) cameras keep watch in such places as streets, banks, shops and factories. In cities, television cameras help control traffic at busy junctions. Traffic controllers watching screens can adjust the lights at the junctions to help the flow of traffic. People can now use the Internet in all sorts of ways, from shopping and banking to voting. In the future, the heart of many homes will be the communications centre. Its televisions will provide all sorts of information, entertainment and education, and link the family to the world outside. This whole revolution in technology has grown out of the creativity and determination that John Logie Baird showed throughout his life.

Timeline

1884	Paul Nipkow patents the Nipkow disc, used for transmitting an exact image of an object on to a screen.
1888	Birth of John Logie Baird in Helensburgh, Scotland.
1894	Guglielmo Marconi first tries to use radio waves to communicate.
1897	Karl Ferdinand Braun invents the cathode ray tube, which later becomes the basis for the modern television set.
1901	Marconi sends out the first radio signals across the Atlantic.
1904	John Fleming invents the diode valve.
1906	Lee de Forest invents the triode valve.
1907	Boris Rosing demonstrates the use of the cathode ray tube as a television receiver.
1908	Campbell Swinton suggests the basic principles of modern electronic television.
1925	Baird gives the first public demonstration of television, in Selfridge's department store in London. Charles Jenkins, in the USA, gives one of the earliest demonstrations of low-definition television. Baird makes the first television transmission of the human face.
1926	Demonstrates 'Noctovision'.
1927	Television images are transmitted by wire between New York and New Jersey by the Bell Telephone Laboratories. Formation of the Baird Television Company.
1928	Baird transmits pictures from London to Hartsdale, New York, USA, via Coulsdon in Surrey, England.
1929	In London, the BBC and the Baird Television Company start the first regular experimental transmission of low-definition pictures.
1930	The first television sets are built and sold in London for £18 each.
1931	Baird marries Margaret Albu in New York.
1932	EMI patents the 'Emitron' electronic camera tube. Birth of Baird's daughter, Diana, in September.
1935	The Selsdon Commission reports its findings. Birth of Baird's son, Malcolm, in July.
1936	The BBC begins operating the first clear black-and-white television service from London.
1937	The BBC chooses the electronic television system. Baird's mechanical television company is closed down. Baird forms a new company, Cinema Television Ltd.

1939	The BBC shuts down all television broadcasting at the outbreak of the Second World War.
1940	Baird patents 'Telechrome', electronic colour television.
1946	Baird's Super TV set is demonstrated. Baird himself misses the demonstration due to illness.
	Death of John Logie Baird on 14 June.

Places to visit and further reading

Places to visit
The Science Museum, London
Museum of the Moving Image (MOMI), London
Museum of Science and Industry, Manchester
The National Museum of Photography, Film and Television, Bradford
Cité des Sciences et de l'Industrie, Paris, France
National Museum of American History, Washington, DC, USA

Websites
Science Museum Homepage:
   www.nmsi.ac.uk
European Collaborative for Science, Industry and Technology Exhibitions:
   www.ecsite.net

Further reading
Hoare, Stephen: *Digital Revolution* – Twentieth Century Inventions series (Hodder Wayland, London, 1998)
Oxlade, Chris: *Light and Sound* – Science Topics series (Heinemann Library Oxford, 1999)
Self, David: *Television* – Media Focus series (Heinemann Library, Oxford, 1998)
Shuter, Jane: *Communications* – A Century of Change series (Heinemann Library, Oxford, 1999)
Shuter, Jane: *Space and Technology* – A Century of Change series (Heinemann Library, Oxford, 1999)

Glossary

amplifying valve electronic valve used to increase the power of electrical signals

apprentice someone who works for a skilled or qualified person in order to learn a trade or craft

associateship position in which someone is joined with others in a business or enterprise

broadcast transmit programmes on radio or television

cathode ray tube vacuum tube in which a beam of electrons is focused onto a flourescent screen to give a spot of light

definition measure of the clarity of a television image as shown by its sharpness and contrast

digital television television system in which the image is transmitted in the form of a numbered code, giving a much clearer picture

diode valve glass valve which is used to convert radio waves into electrical signals that can be transmitted over long distances

diploma document that states someone has gained a qualification or award

electromagnetic wave magnetic field generated by an electric current that spreads out in waves

electronic television system that uses electrons to make television work

element substance that cannot be divided into simpler substances by a chemical reaction. There are just over 100 known elements.

evacuation removal of people from a dangerous place to a safe place until the danger is past, especially during war

high definition television image that is very clear

iconoscope television camera tube in which an electron beam scans the surface, converting an optical image into electrical pulses

Industrial Revolution the process in the 18th and 19th centuries by which Britain and other countries were transformed from agricultural into industrial nations

malaria infectious disease caused by the bite of the mosquito. Symptoms include fever and chills.

mechanical television television system made up of various mechanical and electrical parts

micro-processor tiny wafer or 'chip' of silicon. It contains electrical circuits that do the work of different parts of a computer. Also called 'microchip'

monopoly exclusive control over the manufacture, use and supply of a product or service

Morse code telegraph code used for transmitting messages, in which letters are represented by short dots and longer dashes. Invented by Samuel Morse (1791–1872)

patent the right of a person to make, sell and use an invention they have produced, for a certain period of time

Nipkow disc disc with a spiral pattern of square holes

plasma in physics, a hot ionized gas containing positive ions and electrons

pneumonia inflammation of the lungs that can be life-threatening

Postmaster General head of the postal services in certain countries

Presbyterian Church branch of the Protestant Church, common in Scotland

radio waves pulses of electrical energy that travel through air, space and even solid objects

Royal Commission in Britain, a body set up by the monarch to gather information on any social, educational or other matter

Royal Institution scientific society that was established in Great Britain in 1800

socialist someone who supports socialism, an economic theory or system in which the means of production, distribution and exchange are owned by the community

stereoscopic television a television that produces two-dimensional pictures, giving an illusion of depth

telephone exchange central point where telephone calls are processed

transmitter equipment used for generating and amplifying electrical signals

Index